Orphan to Apprentice:

Child Indentures as Social Welfare

Edited by Siobhan Fitzpatrick

CONTENTS

ACKNOWLEDGMENTS

The exhibit "Orphan to Apprentice: Child Indentures as Social Welfare" would not have been possible without help from several different organizations and individuals. We would like to thank the New Jersey Council for the Humanities, a state partner of the National Endowment for the Humanities, for their grant that enabled us to fund the exhibit, catalog and lecture series. We would also like to acknowledge the support of the Montclair Historical Society and The New-York Historical Society for permitting us to use parts of their wonderful collections in the exhibit. Research for the exhibit was made more enjoyable by the assistance of the librarians at Rose Memorial Library at Drew University. A deep debt of gratitude also goes to our interns at the museum: Michael King, Lauren Rochat, and Jessica Kratovil who assisted with research, exhibit preparation and installation. We would also like to thank our Trustee Thomas Judd for photographing our collection pieces for this catalog. And as always we would like to thank the entire staff at the Museum of Early Trades & Crafts for supporting this project from the beginning.

NEW JERSEY COUNCIL
FOR THE HUMANITIES

Any views, findings, conclusions or recommendations in this publication do not necessarily represent those of the National Endowment for the Humanities or the New Jersey Council for the Humanities.

1. PREFACE

During the eighteenth and nineteenth centuries children who were considered orphans (any child whose father was deceased) or those children whose living circumstances were deemed unfit by the state, were taken from their homes and bound out, or indented, by the local Orphan's Court. While modern audiences often see this practice as barbaric, early contemporary critics considered it a beneficial form of social welfare that helped both the child and state. An orphaned child, who lacked the financial support and guidance of a father, would not have learned a trade and would forever have labored for others, falling lower and lower in society. However, if the child were indented he might learn a trade, as well as reading and writing, and be well set up to start life as a useful member of society when he came of age at twenty-one. The state, of course, benefited from this course of events as well- with the child bound out they no longer had to pay for his full support and there was hope that they would not have to pay for his support as an adult in a prison or an almshouse. In ideal circumstances this system was beneficial.

Apprenticeship required strict compliance from those orphans who were indented. They could not share trade secrets, gamble, drink, marry, or leave without permission (See Fig. 1.1). Yet apprenticeship often came with added benefits, including learning a trade, reading and writing, housing, food and a stable environment, and even at times a cash gift upon termination (See Fig. 1.2). But circumstances were rarely ideal, and often failed to take into account living mothers or other relatives, cruel masters who failed to uphold their part of the agreement, waning trades, and judges who did not keep track of the children once they were placed. The exhibit "Orphan to Apprentice: Child Indentures as Social Welfare," presented by the Museum of Early Trades and Crafts, explores these issues

Fig. 1.1 Shows artifacts related to gambling such as cards, dice and dice cups, as well as those related to drinking including a wine bottle, corkscrew and two horn cups.

through the lives of five orphans: Nelson, John, Peter, Joseph and Sarah.

The three essays that follow explore in-depth several of the topics that the exhibit discusses. Diane Marano's essay, "The Out-of-Place Child: The State's Right to Intervene in Private Affairs," discusses the legal history of government intervention within the family setting with regards to childcare. She clearly demonstrates the precedents set within New Jersey for the practice of indenting orphaned and impoverished children. Carol J. Singley takes a different approach in her essay, "Neither Indentured nor Adopted: Harriet Wilson's *Our Nig*." Singley discusses the ways in which indentures and adoption were meant to be mutually beneficial for the children and their new families but often fell short, especially when issues of race arose. She focuses on the book

Our Nig; or, Sketches from the Life of a Free Black, In A Two-Story White House,

Fig. 1.2 While a master need not give an apprentice a cash gift upon termination it was a welcome gift that could help an apprentice establish himself.

North by Harriet Wilson, the first book by an African American woman, and a semi-autobiographical piece that details the abuse Frado, a mulatto girl, suffers at the hands of a northern family. *Our Nig* would have been available to New Jersey readers and serves as a excellent point of discussion for the role of literature impacting public opinion and practice. In the final essay "Bound to the Hearth: The Role of Gender Norms in the Placement of Orphan Girls" Siobhan Fitzpatrick focuses on the role gender played in determining how beneficial the practice of indenting was to orphaned girls. The need to uphold gender norms of the eighteenth and nineteenth century required Justices of the Peace to treat orphaned girls who passed through their courts differently from boys even when laws, including those in New Jersey, required equal treatment.

These three essays expand our understanding of the connections between child indentures and further explore these topics within New Jersey's history. This research only scratches the surface- there is far more research to be done and more to learn about New Jersey and the rest of the country's orphans, and their treatment during the eighteenth and nineteenth centuries.

2. THE OUT-OF-PLACE CHILD: THE STATE'S RIGHT TO INTERVENE IN PRIVATE AFFAIRS

BY DIANE MARANO

In the eighteenth and nineteenth centuries, as today, the appropriate nature and scope of social interventions with children and adolescents was an important public issue, as well as an issue of critical consequence to the families and children whose lives were touched by such interventions. In New Jersey and in other states, governments addressed fundamental social questions that affected children's lives in significant ways: What was the child's place in society? How were children viewed, and what responsibility should the government take for their care and control? When was it considered proper for the state to intervene in the life of the child by placing her or him with another family? What were the child's responsibilities? What were the new family's responsibilities?

Legislative Framework

Early New Jersey laws reveal that the state's right to intervene in private affairs was premised on legislators' concern for the welfare of both individuals and the community at large. In particular, the practice of employing child indenture as a form of social welfare was rooted in a combination of humanitarian, moral, and practical concerns.

For example, a 1799 New Jersey statute provided that if a parent was viewed as a beggar, common drunkard, or other undesirable type of person, or if a parent did not provide for a child, the child could be bound out "as a servant or apprentice to any person, who may be willing to take such child, till the age of twenty-one years, if a male, or eighteen years, if a female, or for a less time."[1]

This statute, which had the potential to drastically change the life of a child, was included under the section of the laws dealing with disorderly persons. The category of parents whose children could be bound out, or placed under a legal obligation to serve another person, included vagrants, a term which meant persons without a visible means of lawful support who were viewed as able to work.[2] In other words, the children of a poor person who was unemployed could be taken away from their parents and sent to work for "any person who may be willing to take such child." All that was required was for two justices of the peace to agree that the parent was able to work but did not do so, or that the parent was unfit in some other way. The pejorative nature of the language employed by the drafters of this statute makes it clear that, in addition to a financial evaluation, a moral judgment was to be made about the parent's fitness by the justices of the peace.

Unlike the disorderly persons statute, New Jersey's 1846 Poor Law included the word "indenture" to describe the agreement according to which the child was to serve his or her new master or mistress. "Poor Laws" referred to that part of the law which related to the public relief, or support, of paupers,[3] and the placement of the provision for child indentures in New Jersey's

Poor Law demonstrates that a key basis for the system of child indentures was to provide a means for the support of poor children that did not require the public to bear the financial burden of that support.   The term "indenture" was a synonym for a "contract", and the indenture stated the period of time that the child's service was to last. Under this statute, the same time period of service as that provided in the disorderly persons law, up to age twenty-one for a boy or age eighteen for a girl, was permitted. This law also described several different types of circumstances that could lead to a child's being bound out. The local authorities of the town or county were:

> enjoined and commanded to put forth and bind out any poor child or children who have no parents, or whose parents shall apply to the said overseer or overseers for relief, or the child or children of any poor parents whatsoever, who shall bring up their said children in sloth, idleness, and ignorance . . . [4]

Therefore orphaned children, children whose parents applied for relief, or what we would today call public assistance, or children whose poor parents were regarded as raising them improperly could all be bound out as indentured servants. Just as poor adults who "shall live idle, or not engage in some honest employment" were viewed as disorderly persons who could be imprisoned in the workhouse at hard labor for up to three months,[5] poor children whom the authorities believed were being raised in sloth and idleness risked being bound out until they were no longer minors. With both adults and children expected to be engaged in some legitimate business when they were on the streets, the legal atmosphere was not friendly to idlers or wanderers of any age, if they were poor. All in all, children of poor parents who were neither at home, at work, nor at school, although the public school system was still developing during this period, could be viewed as suspicious or dangerous "idlers" who were out of place in the streets and in need of social intervention.

Focusing on the Welfare of the Child

The justification for public authorities to assert their power over children and families was expressed by government representatives outside the legislature as well. In the early nineteenth century, private institutions called Houses of Refuge were established as another form of social welfare for children, and a Philadelphia case from 1838 illustrates how courts of that time supported the state's right to intervene in family affairs. Displaying a moralistic tone similar to that shown by the New Jersey legislature, the Supreme Court of Pennsylvania refused to return a girl named Mary Ann Crouse to her father, who had requested that she be released from the Philadelphia House of Refuge:

> The object of the charity is reformation, by training its inmates to industry; by imbuing their minds with principles of morality and religion; by furnishing them with means to earn a living; and, above all, by separating them from the corrupting influence of improper associates. To this end may not the natural parents, when unequal to the task of education, or unworthy of it, be superseded by the *parens patriae*, or common guardian of the community? It is to be remembered that the public has a paramount interest in the virtue and knowledge of its members, and that of strict right, the business of education belongs to it. That parents are ordinarily entrusted with it is because it can seldom be put into better hands; but where they are incompetent or corrupt, what is there to prevent the public from withdrawing their faculties, held, as they obviously are, at its sufferance?[6]

The court, in asserting that Mary Ann's parents were unequal to the task of educating her, "unworthy", "incompetent", and "corrupt", claimed the community's right to take guardianship of her for the sake of both the child and the public at large. The court maintained that the public had a "paramount interest" in seeing that Mary Ann was brought up in "virtue and knowledge", and furnished with the means to earn a living. Thus, the public good, as well as the good of the child, were viewed as outweighing the parent's right to custody of Mary Ann. The court concluded that there was nothing unconstitutional about restraining a child in a way that would "conduce to an infant's welfare", and ended by declaring:

> The infant has been snatched from a course which must have ended in confirmed depravity; and not only is the restraint of her person lawful, but it would be an act of extreme cruelty to release her from it.

The doctrine of *parens patriae* announced by the Pennsylvania court held that the State, as the guardian of the community, had both the right and the duty to intervene in family affairs on behalf of children. This formulation of the State's affirmative duty to ensure the welfare of children became widely adopted by public bodies to justify not only practices that had already been in place for some time, such as child indentures, but also new forms of intervention with families.

Fig. 2.1 All children would have been taught basic grammar, but only a few would have the opportunity to learn advanced mathematics such as bookkeeping.

The court considered the child's education to be among the central objectives of her upbringing. Pursuing a similar public policy, the New Jersey legislature required that indenture agreements provide "that every such master and mistress to whom such poor child or children shall be bound out as aforesaid, shall cause every such child or children to be taught to read and write" (See Fig.2.1).[7] By imposing this requirement, the legislature sought to ensure that the child would receive at least the most basic education.

In addition, the same law sought to provide for the safety and welfare of the indentured child by appointing the authorities who ordered the child bound out to serve as the child's guardians. In this role, the guardians were required not only to see that the terms of the indenture were performed and fulfilled, but also to "take care . . . that he, she or they be not abused or ill used." In order to enable the authorities to carry out their responsibility to protect the child from harm during the term of the indenture, the guardians were "empowered and directed to inquire into the same, and to redress any such grievance or grievances in such method as the law hath proscribed." Thus the guardians were authorized both to investigate on their own initiative, and also to respond to any complaints that the child might have about how he or she was being treated.

Indirect Pathways into Indentured Service

These New Jersey laws provided for a child to be placed into indentured service directly from parental custody, if indeed the child had parents, but a child might also experience intermediate stops before an indentured placement could be found. Such temporary placements could be either within the public sphere or in private institutions, with the latter becoming more frequent as the nineteenth century progressed and programs like the Houses of Refuge proliferated.

In the public realm, Salem County had established its own system for relief of the poor, consisting of a poorhouse in which not only adults, but also children, were contained. The 1839-1840 version of the Salem Poor Law provided that orphans, children whose parents had applied for relief, and poor parents' children being brought "up in sloth, idleness, and ignorance" were to be brought to the poorhouse, "there to be employed and supported until they can be put forth and bound out as apprentices to suitable places."[8] As the language of the statute indicates, Salem County's poorhouse could also properly be called a county workhouse, as children sent there were to be "employed and supported" in that place until they could be bound out.

Fig. 2.2 Farm equipment was often large, unwieldy and dangerous for young small children.

In the private realm, institutions organized by charitable entities also cared for children until indentured placements could be located for them. New York City and Philadelphia both opened Houses of Refuge in the 1820s, and children from those institutions were sometimes indentured in New Jersey as well. The case of one thirteen year-old African American boy shows that, in addition to the statutory avenues already discussed, children could also be self-referred for placement. This young man, who had been working as a cabin boy on a ship that sailed into New York harbor, jumped ship when he feared his captain was about to sell him into slavery. The boy arrived at the New York House of Refuge in the 1840s, and from there was indentured to a New Jersey farmer who reported back to the House of Refuge that he was very happy with the boy's work and conduct (See Fig. 2.2).[9] Since the voice of the child is so often absent from these historical accounts, however, it is impossible to know whether the boy was as happy as his master with his new life as an indentured servant on a New Jersey farm.

This institution's superintendent kept good records which showed that many children were successfully indentured, while others returned because of problems with their placements. Several young girls, who had been trained in domestic skills during their time at the New York House of Refuge, came back to the Home following their placements as domestic servants. A Mary Shaw returned because of "bad treatment" from the lady of the house to which she was assigned, and a Mary Gash was ill used by her master.[10]

The records of a random sample of 135 African American children who resided at the New York House of Refuge between 1840 and 1900 showed that 82 had been indentured, 37 discharged to relatives, 8 discharged to other institutions, 3 had died, and 5 fell into the category of "other". Of those who had been indentured, the girls seemed to be somewhat more successful than the boys. Out of the 82 children, 57 were boys, of whom 16 were successfully indentured. Twice as many, 32, were failed indentures, and the outcomes of 9 were unknown. Of the 25 indentured girls, 12 were successful, 7 were not, and 6 had unknown outcomes.[11]

Beginning with Trenton's Union Industrial Home for Destitute Children, opened in 1859,[12] New Jersey's religious and charitable organizations likewise opened a number of institutions, both to house children and to place them as indentured servants and apprentices. The Civil War, which left many families ruptured, spurred the opening of many of these Homes, including the Camden Home for Friendless Children in 1865. Its Articles of Incorporation provided that it would receive:

> Children under twelve voluntarily surrendered by their father or, if dead or absent, their mother or guardian, children under twelve committed by the court or the mayor on account of vagrancy, or the exposure, or the neglect, or abandonment of said children by their parents,

those statutory poor children . . . [13]

As the language of its Articles of Incorporation suggests, this Home took in the same children, including those considered to be "vagrant" because they wandered about the streets and the "statutory poor children" defined in the Poor Law, that were required to be bound out under the New Jersey law. The Camden Home's 1867 Annual Report describes the procedure to be followed for binding out the "statutory poor children", providing that:

> These children shall be educated and may, when in the discretion of the managers and trustees, it shall appear proper, bind the said children, <u>with their consent</u>, as apprentices during their minority [to learn a trade or to have such employment as] will be the most conducive to the benefit and advantage of such children.[14] (emphasis supplied)

It is notable that this program maintained that it would only bind a child out after the trustees had determined that it was in the child's best interest and with the child's consent, perhaps suggesting that these Homes, or at least this one, provided an opportunity for their "friendless children" to be somewhat insulated from the potential harshness of the child indenture system as established by New Jersey's laws.

The children who were placed by these Homes were sometimes caught in a tug-of-war between the agencies and their natural parents. The New Jersey Children's Home Society was sued at the end of the nineteenth century by a mother from Paterson who wanted her three children back. Mrs. Murray had previously had a drinking problem, according to the Home Society, but had since reformed, according to a Reverend McNulty, who was supporting the legal action on the mother's behalf. Her children, meanwhile, had already been indentured with private families.[15] This example illustrates that there can be several sides to the custody issue, raising such questions as whether the termination of the parent's rights was permanent, and, if not, which placement the court should consider to be in the best interest of the children.

Immigrant Status, Ethnicity, and Religion

By the 1840s, many areas in the northeastern United States had been flooded with immigrants, including those from Ireland, who were viewed with disdain by many native-born Americans. Moreover, while Catholics had long lived in America, the Irish immigrants' religion became a marker of their low social class and ethnicity. Because the Irish Catholic culture was viewed by some as inferior and criminogenic, one attempted avenue of social rehabilitation was the placement of urban Catholic children in rural Protestant homes, where it was hoped that the children would lose their immigrant culture and imbibe the values of Protestant, rural America.[16] The New Jersey Children's Home Society, the object of Mrs. Murray's legal action in the preceding paragraph, was one institution that pursued this strategy.

Situating Child Indenture Policy in the Context of Social Welfare

As stated above, the system of social welfare in which the child indenture was embedded attempted to balance humanitarian, moral, and practical objectives. On the one hand, the poor were those who were "dependent either on the charity of the general public or on maintenance at the expense of the public."[17] Historically, the fear of increasing the dependency of the poor on public assistance has influenced Anglo-American welfare policy.[18] At times the public's hostility toward the practice of providing public relief, and the fear that relief payments were encouraging pauperism, have prompted proposals to simply abolish relief altogether.[19] This fear and hostility long ago gave rise to an approach, on the part of both the public and lawmakers, of dividing the poor into the categories of the "deserving poor" and the "undeserving poor". Those poor people viewed as deserving were more likely to receive maintenance at the public expense. As the judgmental language of the early New Jersey statutes shows, the New Jersey legislature attempted to criminalize those poor parents branded as "undeserving", deny them public relief, and take away their children. In this way, the moral and legal condemnation of those regarded as the undeserving poor also served the practical purpose of keeping down the public burden of relief payments. The social welfare policies of the eighteenth and nineteenth centuries simultaneously sought to support the poor, to regulate them[20] and, in some ways, to punish them.

At the same time, the children of the poor were viewed as vulnerable and not responsible for their economic circumstances, permitting them to be viewed as deserving of help.[21] This humanitarian impulse was tempered by the belief that many poor children, by virtue of their improper upbringing as well as their neediness, were headed for lives of "confirmed depravity", as the court said of Mary Ann Crouse. These children were seen as "pre-delinquents", simultaneously vulnerable and threatening. Enoch Wines expressed a widely-held belief in 1880 when he described lower-class children as destitute, vagrant, depraved, ragged and filthy. He maintained that these children were "born to crime, brought up for it. They must be saved."[22] Sometimes, if a child's poor parents were viewed as undeserving of receiving what was called "outside assistance", or public support that would permit the family to remain in their home, an indentured placement for the child would be viewed as a way of saving the child from a life of crime or immorality.

Child indentures had been employed since colonial times

as one of several forms of social welfare for the poor. As time went on, however, other factors in addition to class became influential in shaping decisions by local authorities about whether a child should be supported in his or her own home or bound out as an indentured servant. With waves of poor immigrants arriving in northeastern cities during the nineteenth century, race, ethnicity, religion, immigrant status, and gender all became relevant both to the decision about what form of social welfare would be offered to a child, and how an indentured child would be received in her new home.

In this evolving system, child indenture served the public welfare by keeping down the number of people who were supported by public or private charity. It also provided a supply of young workers for those who needed them at a time when child labor was not frowned upon, and was often viewed as benefiting both the child and society by removing the child from the presumed bad influence of the failed parents. Out-of-place children, whether plucked from the streets by police or social welfare agents, delivered into the system by their own parents, or self-referred, found varying degrees of success in their new surroundings. A good placement, however, provided a child with a safe environment, a moral upbringing, a basic education, and training in an agricultural, domestic, or trade skill.

Notes:

[1] Statutes of the State of New Jersey (Phillips & Boswell: Trenton, 1847) 565
[2] Henry Campbell Black, *Black's Law Dictionary, Fourth Edition* (St. Paul, Minn.: West Publishing Company, 1968), 1719
[3] Black's Law Dictionary, 1322
[4] New Jersey Statutes 1847, 883
[5] New Jersey Statutes 1847, 564-565

[6] *Ex Parte Crouse*, 4 Wharton 9, 11 (Pa. 1838)

[7] New Jersey Statutes 1847, 884

[8] New Jersey Statutes 1847, 897-898

[9] G.S. Gupta, "Black and 'Dangerous'?: African American Working Poor Perspectives on Juvenile Reform and Welfare in Victorian New York, 1840-1900" (*The Journal of Negro History*, 86(2), 2001), 99

[10] A.W. Pisciotta, "Treatment on Trial: The Rhetoric and Reality of the New York House of Refuge, 1857-1935", (American Journal of Legal History, 29, 151-181, 1985), 168

[11] Gupta. "Black and 'Dangerous'?", 125

[12] Union Industrial Home for Children, 140th Anniversary Dinner Report (Trenton, New Jersey: Union Industrial Home for Children, 2000)

[13] Camden Home for Friendless Children, 1867 Annual Report, 7-8

[14] Camden Home for Friendless Children, 1867 Annual Report, 8

[15] "Mother Wants Children Back", *New York Times*, January 8, 1900,7.(http://proquest.umi.com.proxy.libraries.rutgers.edu/pqdweb?)

[16] Schneider, Eric C., *In the Web of Class: Delinquents and Reformers in Boston, 1810s-1930s (New York: New York University Press, 1992),* 55

[17] Black's Law Dictionary, 1322

[18] Schneider, *In the Web of Class,* 1

[19] Frances Fox Piven, and Richard A. Cloward, *Regulating the Poor: The Functions of Public Welfare*(New York: Vintage Books, 1971) 150

[20] Piven & Cloward, *Regulating the Poor,*

[21] Schneider, *In the Web of Class,* 26

[22] Anthony M. Platt, The Child Savers: The Invention of Delinquency (Chicago, Illinois: University of Chicago Press, 1969), frontispiece

3. NEITHER INDENTURED NOR ADOPTED: HARRIET WILSON'S *OUR NIG*

BY CAROL J. SINGLEY

This essay examines the intersections of indentured service and adoption as they appear in the first African-American novel by a woman, *Our Nig*, by Harriet Nelson published in 1859. Adoption and indentured service are not identical forms of care, but they share characteristics: that of providing food, shelter, and training for children and offering mutual benefit, at least in theory, to children and their adoptive parents or masters. In some cases, indentured contracts were de facto adoption papers, and the indenture experience tantamount to adoption. In nineteenth-century literature, both adoption and indentured service are the means by which the child can become assimilated, and often find his or her social and economic status improved, through relationship with a more affluent family. The family, in turn, is helped by the presence and participation of the indentured or adopted child. The exchange of labor is central to the terms of indenture; labor in the form of selfless service also appears in nineteenth-century literature about adoption, in which one measure of the child's success is worthiness demonstrated through obedience and cheerful helpfulness. The adopted child supports the

Reprinted with permission from chapter 6, "Servitude and Homelessness: Harriet Wilson's Our Nig," in _Adopting America: Childhood, Kinship and National Identity in Literature_ (New York: Oxford University Press, 2011), pp. 119-34.

family as an expansive, flexible, and aspiring unit, paralleling the ideology of the United States as an expansive nation.

In popular mid-nineteenth century novels such as Susan Warner's *The Wide, Wide World* (1850) and Susanna Maria Cummins's *The Lamplighter* (1854), white middle-class authors use the adoption plot to advance a domestic version of the nineteenth-century American dream. Adoption into a loving family or its alternative, reunion with the family of origin, affirms familial and social cohesion

Fig. 3.1 Adopted children would have more of a modern childhood with handmade toys like the top as well as manufactured family games like Tiddledy Winks.

at a time when society was confronting the unsettling effects of immigration, urbanization, and capitalism. These domestic novels extend the notion of the white bourgeois family outward to mutually reinforcing notions of a growing nation (See Fig. 3.1).[1] Tales of indentured service similarly provide blueprints for upward mobility and success.[2] However, the system of adoption or indenture did not serve all children. Its failure to meet the needs of African Americans is vividly demonstrated in Wilson's autobiographical novel. As critic Amy Schrager Lang writes, "the orphaned Frado suffers from a homelessness that nothing, it seems, can assuage."[3]

Wilson's antebellum novel tells the story of a mixed race girl who is abandoned by her impoverished mother. Left on the doorstep of a white Northern family's home, Frado Smith is taken in and exploited for her labor. There is no happy ending for Frado, either through adoption or reunification with her birth family, as there is for countless white children featured in domestic novels. *Our Nig* demonstrates the abuses of indentured service and the limits of adoption for a poor, racially marked Northern child deemed unfit for the middle class. In this scathing indictment of nineteenth-century child welfare, indentured service is not redemptive but tortuous, leading not to opportunity and success but to debilitation and despair.

Indenturing has a long history in the United States, beginning in colonial times. As a general practice, it dates far earlier. John Boswell claims that in ancient and medieval Europe, most abandoned children were taken in by adults for the purposes of extracting work from them.[4] The American system of indentured service, most representative in the Chesapeake colonies, served a variety of needs. It offered shelter, food, and clothing to poor, illegitimate, and orphaned children who might otherwise become burdens on the community. It also provided labor while giving the indentured individual purposeful work, skills, and improved religious and moral character.

Indentured service was a traditional solution to the problem of orphaned, abandoned, or destitute children in New England.[5] New England practices were similar to those in other regions except that New England colonists, both practical and influenced by the Calvinist doctrine of Election, took care to prevent burdensome individuals from entering their ranks or weeded them out in an attempt to reduce the number of people requiring town assistance.[6] Indentured children did not assume the name of their master, nor were they given inheritance rights. The responsibility of the master ended when the child reached adulthood and received the proverbial $50, a Bible, and two suits of clothing (See Fig. 3.2).[7]

Fig. 3.2 Traditional termination gifts included a new suit of clothing, a Bible and a monetary reward.

In decline by 1830,[8] indenturing was still practiced in some states well into the twentieth century[9] and remained in legal use until 1917.[10] The practice of "putting out" orphaned or poor children with childless couples or families needing labor continued on a large scale in the United States with orphan trains, organized by Charles Loring Brace. These trains transported indigent and orphaned children without indenture contracts from New York City to Midwestern and Western farm families from the 1860s to the early 1900s.[11] Some of these children were legally adopted by families and lovingly cared for, but others labored in exchange for food and shelter and experienced varying degrees of abuse or neglect.

At the beginning of the twentieth century, the understanding of childhood gradually changed from "productive" to "priceless." Until then, it was expected that children taken in by families would contribute to the household.[12] These arrangements afforded opportunities for exploitation, a fact that Progressive-era reformers acknowledged when they disparagingly referred to indentured servitude as "binding-out," connecting it to "the days when slavery and serfdom were tolerated."[13] Indeed, the practice left many children vulnerable and put female children, in particular, at risk of sexual abuse.

In *Our Nig*, Frado's "unofficial indenture," as Gretchen Short writes, is "informed by a long tradition going back to the colonial New England of the seventeenth century which practiced a kind of militantly exclusionary domesticity."[14] It is consistent with nineteenth-century attitudes toward child placement and labor and is resonant with Wilson's own experience as a domestic servant, which informs Frado's trials at the Bellmonts'. Wilson would have begun working for the Hayward family around 1830, when the practice still had currency.[15] She was likely abused by the family for whom she worked.[16] Frado is similarly confined and severely beaten, possibly raped,[17] and her skin darkened to accentuate her blackness.

Indeed, Wilson shows a close connection between the indentured service of African Americans and slavery. The indenturing of *all* people has been decried as a form of slavery, although the practice continued for some years after slavery's abolition.[18] African-American children were especially affected during the antebellum period, when few options existed for the homeless. The Colonial Orphan Asylum, founded in 1836, was the first orphanage for African-American children, but asylums were not readily available for African-American orphans and orphans of other racial and ethnic minorities until the late nineteenth century.[19] African-American children were often considered ineligible for adoption; it was not until well into the twentieth century, with the 1948 Child Welfare League of America Conference on Adoption, that any significant headway was made in expanding the definition of adoptable child to include African Americans or other minorities, or disabled, older, or foreign-born children.[20] Since the colonial days, in lieu of institutional support, African-American children were raised in their own communities in extended families, where children born out of wedlock were less stigmatized than white children were in their social groups.[21] Frado, however, is alienated from both the white and African-American communities and benefits from none of these supports.

American literature provides accounts of indentured service and offers insight into the role of race in setting its terms. For example, Puritan preacher Cotton Mather owned slaves and housed a Spanish-Indian girl servant. He was by no means an abolitionist, yet he denounced the brutal aspects of the colonial slave trade and asked Boston residents to examine their consciences and consider whether slaves are "always treated according to the Rules of Humanity? . . . Are they treated as those, that are of one Blood with us?"[22] In *The Negro Christianized* (1706), he reminded slaveowners that "'They are *Men*, and not *Beasts* that you bought.'"[23] Emphatic on the issue of religion, Mather cared deeply about the spiritual well-being of those dependent upon him, unlike the Bellmonts, who actively discourage Frado's practice of religion.[24]

American literature also provides accounts of indentured service from the servant's perspective. Elizabeth Sampson Sullivan Ashbridge (1713–55) was born in England, married at age fourteen and widowed a few months later. She embarked alone for Pennsylvania, intending to locate her mother's brother, but instead she found herself bound as an indentured servant without fully knowing what her contract entailed. As she describes being coerced to sign a four-year contract to pay for the transatlantic crossing: "were it possible to convey in characters a scene of the sufferings of my servitude, it would affect the most stony heart with pity for a young creature who had been so tenderly brought up."[25]

Both Ashbridge and Frado are unwillingly indentured, endure physical abuse, and struggle to keep religious faith. Ashbridge writes that her master "was so inhuman that he would not suffer me to have clothes to be decent in, making me to go barefoot in the snowy weather."[26] Frado suffers not cold but heat when Mrs. Bellmont orders her hatless so that the sun darkens her skin and exaggerates her difference from the Bellmont family: "Mrs. Bellmont was determined the sun should have full power to darken the shade which nature had first bestowed upon her as best befitting."[27] Ashbridge expresses disgust at the hypocrisy of a master who denigrates her while praying and taking the sacrament. Wilson likewise sarcastically refers to Mrs. Bellmont as a "professor of religion," who forbids Frado to attend church, claiming that "religion was not meant for niggers."[28]

Both Ashbridge and Frado struggle with their faith as a result of their ordeals. Ashbridge begins to "believe there was no such a thing as religion."[29] Frado likewise believes that "she was unfit for any heaven, made for whites or blacks"[30] and rejects a God who made the Bellmont women white and her black.[31] Despite abuse, Ashbridge concludes her narrative by affirming Christian faith. Frado likewise ends by "reposing on God [with whom] she has thus far journeyed securely"[32] although she enjoys few comforts associated with piety or church membership.

Nineteenth-century debate over the servant's place in U.S. society revealed a conflict between democratic ideals and an entrenched perception of deserved Anglo-European hegemony. "A servant," Harriet Beecher Stowe wrote, "can never in our country be the mere appendage to another man; . . . he must be a fellow-citizen, with an established position of his own, free to make contracts, free to come and go, and having in his sphere titles to consideration and respect just as definite as those of any trade or profession whatever."[33] At the time, Stowe was concerned with fair treatment of the Irish servant class, which she deemed essential not only for domestic harmony but also for American republican ideals of equality and democracy. However, her egalitarianism had distinct limits. Her "projected assimilation of Irish servants into American domestic economy . . . is not an option for emancipated slaves," as Gillian Brown notes, citing Topsy in *Uncle Tom's Cabin* as an illustration of a black child who remains outside the orbit of "sentimental possession."[34]

By the mid-nineteenth century, religious sentiments congealed around national pride built on a sense of the republic's past as well as its future. However, a collective cultural genealogy worked against the welfare of black and mulatto children such as Frado, who were of uncertain and scorned lineage. Even Horace Bushnell, noted proponent of childhood nurture, makes heritage a condition of godliness. In his well-regarded book, *Christian Nurture*, he affirms that some races are disadvantaged because they do not have the "long continuance" of the "qualities of education, habit, feeling, and character" that over time "become thoroughly inbred in the [Anglo] stock."[35] Lacking this continuity, Frado must depend on the Bellmonts' nonexistent sense of fairness.

Harriet Wilson relies on the conventions of indentured service to narrate Frado's ordeal of Northern racism, sexism, and classism.[36] As Elizabeth Breau notes, the fact that Frado "is not even legally indentured; she is bound by default," allows Wilson to voice outrage "that slavery, or its partner, indentured servitude, can exist among those who congratulate themselves on their moral superiority to Southern slaveholders."[37] The novel's subtitle reminds readers that Frado is technically free but virtually enslaved: "A Two-Story White House, North Showing that Slavery's Shadows Fall Even There." As Wilson asserts in her preface, Frado's "mistress was wholly imbued with *southern principles*" (n.b., original emphasis). When Frado's mother fails to return for Frado after leaving her, ostensibly for the day, the Bellmonts must decide what to do with their new charge. Mrs. Bellmont declares, "[i]f I could make her do my work in a few years, I would keep her,"[38] and Frado is promptly put into service. She is not adopted, nor is her labor legally contracted. Instead, she toils for twelve years without protection or benefit (See Fig. 3.3).

Fig. 3.3 Cooking and baking were traditional "housewifery" skills that apprenticed girls would learn using iron and copper tools.

This tale of indentured service allows Wilson to deliver a scathing critique of race and Northern economic and social relations. Indentured service was a market driven system that usually involved a contract or mutually understood arrangement that delineated the responsibilities and rights of both parties and that ended after a specific period of time, at which point the indentured individual would be free to earn her or his own living.[39] Frado joins the Bellmont household with no such arrangement and for an indefinite period of time. When she leaves, the Bellmonts make a mockery of the custom of giving two suits of clothing, a Bible, and $50 by giving her one suit of clothing, a Bible, and 50 cents. The fact that Frado labors under cruel supervision without remuneration, fails to become self-sufficient, and develops no loving attachment to the Bellmonts makes her service closer to slavery. She leaves their home debilitated, dependent, and unable to support herself. Blurring the lines between putative freedom in the North and institutionalized slavery in the South, Wilson shows that domestic service can be worse than slavery.

In the free North, state legislators usually granted freedom to African Americans who had served in the Revolution; many freed blacks were able to save enough money to purchase the freedom of others. A gradual abolition process in the North allowed others to gain their freedom. However, blacks took their place behind whites economically and socially. Although Northerners upheld a theory of natural rights that powered abolitionist rhetoric, their call to end racial hostility fell far short of egalitarianism. Inheriting an English concept of race, language, and tradition, they maintained a racialized view of society, fearing both the blurred racial lines suggested by miscegenation and competition in the labor market.[40] Deemed unfit for skilled and professional occupations, free blacks were considered naturally "lazy, childlike and immature." A New York merchant even insisted that these laborers be treated as children, under the supervision of adult white guardianship.[41]

Wilson's depiction of a laboring child who is anything but lazy and yet is unable to exert control over her employment or wages once she reaches adulthood constitutes a satiric commentary on the treatment of free blacks in North.[42] As Frado says about the Bellmonts, "they owe me something," but she cannot make them pay. Her dependence on the Bellmonts and seemingly permanent residence with them resemble adoption. However, although she is in need of a home, adoption is never an option, a fact both true of Wilson's time and reflective of adoption practices in the century to follow. Indeed, Wilson anticipates the undesirability of African-American "special needs children" in the twentieth-century public welfare system. Such children, Patricia J. Williams writes, are unwanted and disposable.[43] Frado is nothing more to the Bellmonts than a household "nig." Class and gender play roles in her misfortune, but race trumps both categories. As Frado laments, "I ha' nt got no mother, no home. I wish I was dead"[44]; "No mother, father, brother, or sister to care for me . . .—all because I am black!"[45]

If there is a bright spot in Wilson's tale of neglect and abuse, it is found in the appendices to the novel. Frado's story continues in three letters, each of which describes her plight and progressively points to both race and the power of authorship. Like prefaces to slave narratives, these documents authenticate the author's claims and generate reader sympathy

Fig.3.4 Hat blocks used in shaping hats.

in order to mobilize abolitionist support, but their appearance at the end rather than at the beginning of the text is a "parodic inversion" that underlines Wilson's skill as creative storyteller[46] and reinforces her point that even though Frado has reached adulthood, she is still like a child in need of a home. In the first appendix, a writer identified as "Allida" explains that Frado is finally "adopted" by a kindly woman, Mrs. Walker, who takes her in, nurses her through illness, and helps her obtain work as a hat maker (See Fig. 3.4 and 3.5). But when Frado

Fig. 3.5 Presses used for creating artificial flowers for decorating hats.

falls in love, marries, and is deserted by her husband, she becomes homeless again. She moves to a county poor house, where her son is born in surroundings no better than the attic space to which Frado was consigned with the Bellmonts.

The second appendix, by Margaretta Thorn, acknowledges racism in a way that Allida's preface does not by urging readers "not to look at [i.e, judge] the color of the hair, the eyes, or the skin," and to realize that Frado "was indeed a slave, in every sense of the word."[47] Thorn also credits Frado with another role: that of an author seeking a home for her story as well as for herself. Finding readers for Frado's narrative will be difficult, however, for those who buy her book must also buy her story. That is, they must admit that cruelties such as those committed by the Bellmonts exist in the abolitionist North. They must acknowledge that whereas adoption normally provides a foundation for unbroken lineage of future generations, for Frado or other children living under "slavery's shadows," there is no such genealogical cohesion. Unlike her mother, Frado keeps her child, as did Wilson herself. However, a little more than five months after *Our Nig* is published, the child dies. He was nearly eight, just a little older than Frado was when she arrived at the Bellmonts. With this death, Wilson calls for a different kind of adoption. She asks not white but "colored brethren" to "rally around me a faithful band of supporters and defenders,"[48] adopt her book, and give it a home.

The author of the third appendix, known only by the initials, C. D. S, likewise endorses Frado's book, "hoping that its circulation will be extensive." Because the writer of this appendix says that Frado's "complexion is a little darker than mine" and "esteem[s] it a privilege to . . . assist her whenever an opportunity present itself," Henry Louis Gates deduces that the writer's race is white. However, Gates also notes that "'C. D. S.' was also a *legal* abbreviation for 'Colored Indentured Servant.'"[49] If Wilson intended the latter meaning, she literally uses a mark of indentured service to end her tale.

Wilson draws on conventions of white middle-class adoption narratives and tales of indentured service, but she undermines the sentimental aspects of both experiences. Frado's failures point out the social undesirability and mistreatment of antebellum black and mulatto children, and the lack of protections available for such children. By documenting the cruelty of domestic service for African-American children and exposing the abuse disguised as discipline that these children face, Wilson demonstrates the shallowness of abolitionist rhetoric, for despite putative freedom, Frado is spurned by the white family that can help her and is treated worse than a slave. The felicitous endings found in bourgeois narratives about domestic service and adoption are unavailable to African-American children living in the context of slavery.

Notes:
[1] Although novels such as *The Wide, Wide World* and *The Lamplighter* acknowledge class differences, they do not take race into account. Harriet Beecher Stowe's *Uncle Tom's Cabin* 1852), a notable exception, shows that to be orphaned and black is to be doubly marginalized in a society that privileges whiteness. However, although Ophelia rescues Topsy from slavery and provides housing and education, she cannot bring herself to love Topsy or adopt her. In contrast to Stowe, Wilson explores the workings of kinship, class, *and* race to show the failure of the white abolitionist agenda to serve children most in need.

[2] See, for example, *Bound Out; or Abby at the Farm* by Sarah S. Baker [Sarah Schoonmaker] (1824–1926), in which a young white girl is taken from an orphan asylum and put into service with a farm family. Although the family initially values her only for her labor, Abby's steadfast service and Christian faith help her through adversity, bring about the religious conversion of the family, and result in her adoption. The opposite is true in *Our Nig*, Frustrated at every turn because she is unable to overcome the stigma of her roots and race, Frado remains literally and spiritually orphaned.

[3] Amy Schrager Lang, *The Syntax of Class: Writing Inequality in Nineteenth-Century America* (Princeton, N.J.: Princeton University Press, 2003), 63–64.

[4] John Boswell, *The Kindness of Strangers: The Abandonment of Children in Western Europe from Late Antiquity to the Renaissance* (New York: Pantheon, 1988), 225–27.

[5] Marcus Wilson Jernegan, *Laboring and Dependent Classes in Colonial America, 1607–1783* (Chicago: University of Illinois Press, 1931), 179; Robert Francis Seybolt, *Apprenticeship and Apprenticeship Education in Colonial New England and New York* (New York: Teachers College, Columbia University, 1917), 36, 49; E. Wayne Carp, *Family Matters: Secrecy and Disclosure in the History of Adoption* (Cambrdge, Mass.: Harvard University Press, 1998), 6.

[6] Jernegan, *Laboring and Dependent Classes*, 179, 191–93.

[7] Christine A. Adamec and William L. Pierce, eds., "Introduction," in *The Encyclopedia of Adoption*, 2nd ed. (New York: Facts on File, 2000), xxi.

[8] David W. Galenson, *White Servitude in Colonial America: An Economic Analysis* (New York: Cambridge University Press, 1981) cites the following as reasons for the decline: low levels of English migration, slow economic growth, low costs of transatlantic passage followed by large-scale migration of free workers, and the arrival of Asian, indentured migrants (179–81). See also David Northrup, *Indentured Labor in the Age of Imperialism, 1834–1922* (New York: Cambridge University Press, 1995), 4; and David W. Galenson, "The Rise and Fall of Indentured Servitude in the Americas: An Economic Analysis," *Journal of Economic History* 44(1) (1984): 1–26.

[9] Ellen Herman, *Kinship by Design: A History of Adoption in the Modern United States* (Chicago: University of Chicago Press, 2008), 23.

[10] Galenson, "Rise and Fall of Indentured Servitude," 1.

[11] Carp, *Family Matters*, 9–10.

[12] Herman, *Kinship by Design*, 26. Viviana A. Zelizer describes the movement from productivity to pricelessness in *Pricing the Priceless Child: The Changing Social Value of Children* (New York: Basic Books, 1985).

[13] Herman, *Kinship by Design*, 26.

[14] Gretchen Short, "Harriet Wilson's *Our Nig* and the Labor of Citizenship," *Arizona Quarterly* 57(3)(Autumn) (2001), relates Frado's failure to achieve self-sufficiency and full citizenship through her labor to "domestic imperialism" (8).

[15] See Barbara A. White, who asserts that Wilson was born between 1824 and 1828 and most likely appeared as a "free colored

person" in the Nehemiah Hayward home in the 1840 census of Milford, when she was between ten and twenty-four years old ("'Our Nig' and the She-Devil: New Information about Harriet Wilson and the 'Bellmont' Family," *American Literature* 65(1) [1993]: 22).

[16] White, "'Our Nig,'" 31–32.

[17] See Cassandra Jackson, "Beyond the Page: Rape and the Failure of Genre," in *Harriet Wilson's New England*, ed. Boggis, Raimon, and White, 140; and Ronna C. Johnson, "Said but Not Spoken: Elision and the Representation of Rape, Race, and Gender in Harriet E. Wilson's *Our Nig*," in *Speaking the Other Self: American Women Writers*, ed. Jeanne Campbell Reesman (Athens: University of Georgia Press, 1997), 96–116.

[18] Adamec and Pierce, xxi.

[19] Adamec and Pierce, xxvii–iii. Herman notes in *Kinship by Design* that although the number of asylums proliferated until 1900, children of color needing placement faced exclusion or segregation until the post-1945 era (22).

[20] Carp, *Family Matters*, 32.

[21] Jon Butler, *Becoming America: The Revolution before 1776* (Cambridge, Mass.: Harvard University Press, 2000), 45.

[22] Cotton Mather, *Diary of Cotton Mather*, ed. Worthington Chauncey Ford, *Collections of the Massachusetts Historical Society*, 7th ser., VII–VIII (Boston, 1912), 687, quoted in Kenneth Silverman, *The Life and Times of Cotton Mather* (New York: Harper & Row, 1984), 264.

[23] Cotton Mather, *The Negro Christianized; An essay to excite and assist the good work, the instruction of Negro-servants in Christianity* (Boston: B. Green, 1706), 23; original emphasis, *Early American Imprints, 1639–1800*, first series, no. 1262, http://docs.newsbank.com/s/Evans/eaidoc/EAIX/0F2FD4175B2416 F0/0DC2EA1C6DFCA835 (accessed July 1, 2010).

[24] Silverman, *Life and Times of Cotton Mather*, 290.

[25] Elizabeth Ashbridge, *Some Account of the Fore Part of the Life of Elizabeth Ashbridge* (Nantwich, England: J. Bromley, 1774), in *The Meridian Anthology of Early American Women Writers: From Anne Bradstreet to Louisa May Alcott, 1650–1865*, ed. Katharine M. Rogers

(New York: Penguin, 1991), 113. Although Ashbridge concludes with an affirmation of Christian faith, she chronicles the effect of steady abuse on her spirit.

[26]Ashbridge, 114.

[27] Harriet Wilson, *Our Nig; or, Sketches from the Life of a Free Black, In A Two-Story White House, North*, ed. and introd. Henry Louis Gates (1859; repr., New York: Vintage, 1983), 39.

[28] Wilson, *Our Nig*, 68.

[29] Ashbridge, 114.

[30] Wilson, *Our Nig*, 85.

[31] Ibid., 51.

[32] Ibid., 130.

[33] Harriet Beecher Stowe, "Servants," *House and Home Papers* by Christopher Crowfield [pseud.] (Boston: Ticknor & Fields, 1865), 221, quoted in Gillian Brown, *Domestic Individualism Imagining Self in Nineteenth-Century America* (Berkeley and Los Angeles: University of California Press, 1990), 55.

[34] Brown, *Domestic Individualism*, 55. Brown emphasizes the segregationist aspects of Stowe's reform agenda. In *Uncle Tom's Cabin*, an orphaned black child can become, under the auspices of a well-positioned Northern foster mother, an educated and respectable member of society. However, rather than integrate the mature Topsy into white society, Stowe sends her to Africa to live. Stowe's domestic program is decidedly different for whites and blacks.

[35] Horace Bushnell, *Christian Nurture* (1847; Grand Rapids, Mich.: Baker Book House, 1979), 202.

[36] Wilson also relies on literary conventions of the seduction tale, the slave narrative, and the conversion narrative R. J. Ellis writes that *Our Nig* "fractures generic boundaries" of the sentimental conversion genre in "Body Politics and the Body Politic in William Wells Brown's *Clotel* and Harriet Wilson's *Our Nig*," in *Soft Canons: American Women Writers and Masculine Tradition*, ed. Karen L. Kilcup (Iowa City: University of Iowa Press, 1999), 100. Rachel Carby analyzes the novel as an allegory of the slave narrative in *Reconstructing Womanhood: The Emergence of the Afro-American Woman Novelist* (New York: Oxford University Press), 43. See also Elizabeth J. West, "Reworking the Conversion Narrative: Race

and Christianity in *Our Nig*," *MELUS* 24(2) (1999): 3–27; and Henry Louis Gates, who writes that Wilson "combines the received conventions of the sentimental novel with certain key conventions of the slave narratives, then combines the two into *one new form*" (ed. and introd., *Our Nig* [New York: Random House, 1982], lii; original emphasis).

[37] Elizabeth Breau, "Identifying Satire: *Our Nig*," *Callaloo* 16(2) (1993): 456.

[38] Wilson, Our Nig, 26.

[39] Galenson, *White Servitude*, 97.

[40] Joyce Appleby, *Inheriting the Revolution: The First Generation of Americans* (Cambridge, Mass.: Harvard University Press, 2000), 16, 158–60.

[41] Leon F. Litwack, *North of Slavery: The Negro in the Free States, 1790–1860* (Chicago: University of Chicago Press, 1961), 156; A New York Merchant, *The Negro Labor Question* (New York: J. A. Gray, 1858): 5–6, 21–22, quoted in Litwack, 156.

[42] See Gabrielle Forman's analysis of labor, class structure, and the autobiographical aspects of the novel in "Recovered Autobiographies and the Marketplace: *Our Nig's* Generic Genealogies and Harriet Wilson's Entrepreneurial Enterprise," in *Harriet Wilson's New England*, ed. Boggis, Raimon, and White,123–38.

[43] Patricia J. Williams, *The Rooster's Egg* (Cambridge, Mass.: Harvard University Press, 1995), 223. The history of transracial adoption in the United States reads like a chronicle of race relations. "Matching" the racial, ethnic, and religious qualities of children and adoptive families was the leading principle behind placements throughout most of the twentieth century, when segregation laws and practiced were common. In response to increasing numbers of transracial adoptions and perhaps to the 1965 Moynihan Report, describing the black family as a threatened institution, in 1972 the National Association of Black Social Workers (NABSW) began to defend a policy of placing African American orphans only in African American families. The NABSW defended its policy as protecting the black family and community as a legitimate and viable institution and attacked transracial adoption as a "form of genocide" (Rita James Simon and Howard Altstein, *Transracial Adoption* [New York: Wiley, 1977], 50–52).

These essentialist views see race as a fixed category identical to culture. In 1977, the Interracial Family Association issued a statement defending transracial adoption, but, as Margaret Homans points out, supporters of this practice "still see it as second best after in-racial adoption" ("Adoption and Essentialism," *Tulsa Studies in Women's Literature* 21(2) [2002], 260). Proponents of transracial adoption include Simon and Altstein, *Transracial Adoption*; Elizabeth Bartholet, *Family Bonds: Adoption and the Politics of Parenting* (Boston: Houghton Mifflin, 1993), 86–117. Opponents include Sandra Patton, *BirthMarks: Transracial Adoption in Contemporary America* (New York: New York University Press, 2000), 154–56.

[44] Wilson, *Our Nig*, 46.

[45] Ibid., 75.

[46] Breau, "Identifying Satire," 458.

[47] Wilson, *Our Nig*, 138-139.

[48] Ibid., 3.

[49] Gates, introduction, Wilson, *Our Nig*, xix–xx; original emphasis.

4. BOUND TO THE HEARTH: THE ROLE OF GENDER NORMS IN THE PLACEMENT OF ORPHAN GIRLS

BY SIOBHAN FITZPATRICK

During the eighteenth and nineteenth centuries perceptions of where orphan girls should be placed were heavily influenced by contemporary concepts of the feminine ideal as personified by Republican Motherhood and the "cult of true domesticity." Each of these concepts appeared at different points in history, and each influenced public opinion in slightly different ways, but they did have some common themes. Both reinforced the idea that women were responsible for raising children, and young children in particular, that women needed to remain in the home to properly perform their role in society and by the time the "cult of domesticity" came to rule popular opinion, that women should only be involved in domestic matters and not be concerned with matters outside of their home.[1] The result of these ideals was that most orphaned girls ended up in domestic service so that they could learn the valuable skills needed to be wives and mothers. It was also believed that keeping girls within a family setting would help to protect their virtue, although that was not always the case, as male members of the household frequently victimized domestic servants.[2] For those girls who did not marry, they would be able to use their newly developed skills to find positions as domestic servants, a menial labor position, and one that they would remain in for life. The limited placement options reduced the opportunities that orphan girls had for fully benefiting from the binding out system. Race could also limit a girl's opportunity for successful placement. While girls were typically placed in the same situations regardless of race, they received different treatment within those positions based on race. Euro-American girls typically received the best treatment and the most educational opportunities, and had the greatest chance of marrying up, while African-American girls had little chance of marrying out of their social class and would receive the least education when compared to all orphans.[3]

The placement of orphaned girls took into strict account the traditional gender norms of eighteenth and nineteenth centuries. The expectation was that a girl would marry and become a mother. Her place in turn was inside the family home or at least the family property. Within her role as wife and mother a woman would be expected to perform certain chores including cooking, cleaning, laundry, mending, caring for children and benefitting the family economy whenever possible. While there were women who did not marry or produce children they were seen as the exception to the rule rather than living another possible option. With such a narrow view of what girls would eventually become it is not unusual that many were indented to learn the "Art of Housewifery" rather than a trade.[4]

Fig. 4.1 Sad Irons which needed to be heated in the fire were used for ironing the laundry.

As an apprentice in housewifery, many orphan girls became de facto domestic servants, even if they were not indented as such. As a domestic servant an orphan girl acted as an additional hand around the household, allowing it run more efficiently. She would perform chores traditionally performed by daughters of the house, who either were now married with their own homes, or too young to assist, or if the family was not fortunate enough to have female children.[5] These tasks varied depending upon what type of household in which the girls were placed, but typically included many of the traditional chores that a wife and mother needed to know, such as cooking, cleaning, and childcare (See Figs. 4.1 and 4.2). Many of the older orphan girls would have arrived knowing at least the basics of how to care for a small child, having helped with younger siblings at home, or how to prepare simple meals,

Fig. 4.2 Cooking and baking required long hours and early mornings in order to have meals ready on time.

once again having performed these tasks in their own homes.[6] For those girls who were too young to have learned before they were indented, they would receive valuable skill training that could be used in setting up their own household or in acquiring a position as a paid domestic servant after their apprenticeship ended. While many girls were technically indented out to a male master, their instructor in the "Arts of Housewifery" would not have been the head of the household; rather it would have been his wife, or in a wealthy home potentially the head female servant.[7] While the skills orphan girls learned as domestic servants would be useful as wives and mothers it relegated those who did not, or could not, marry to menial labor positions for the rest of their lives.

The other area that girls might be apprenticed into was textile production. By the nineteenth century the majority of trades associated with fiber, including spinning, needlework, rough weaving and most garment work, had been gendered as female. The extent to which a particular trade was gendered as female depended upon the region. Not all fiber trades were originally considered feminine and many were regionally re-gendered at different rates based on changes in local economies. Within the western European tradition spinning had always been performed by women, with the distaff acting as a traditional feminine symbol throughout the eighteenth and nineteenth century. It was thus considered acceptable to indent orphan girls as "spinsters," meant to learn the art of spinning.[8] Weaving on the other hand has a more varied history- traditionally master weavers were men, although women could act as assistants, and their spinning was essential to creating a finished product. In the middle colonies master weavers created the fine products, but women who had been trained in the basics of weaving began to produce plain cloth, with production eventually shifting to factories, once again first staffed by men and later women.[9] The repeated re-gendering of weaving demonstrates the more fluid nature of trade gendering. Needlework, which includes decorative stitch work, plain garment work, knitting and lace making, have all been considered feminine pursuits within the Euro-American tradition. The changes over time that occur in how these trades are perceived related more to class. While women of all classes would have learned the basics of hand sewing and knitting, those of the upper and middle classes would have learned more

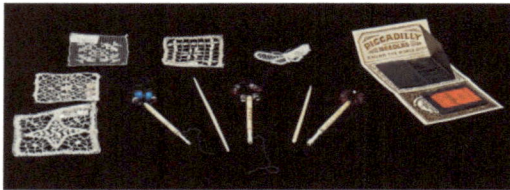

Fig. 4.3 Lace came in a variety of styles and could be made using many different techniques including tatting, bobbin lace and crochet.

decorative stitches as an essential part of their education rather than as a trade skill. The working class girls would have been more likely to develop more skills in garment making as trade skills. Lace making was often taught on a regional basis since it was tied to the family skills (See Fig. 4.3).[10]

Out of all skills that orphaned girls might be apprenticed to learn, or could learn as part of their "housewifery" skills, spinning, weaving and hand sewing were the most practical and useful. All three provided some opportunity for limited financial independence outside of domestic service by the nineteenth century. Spinning and hand sewing could be done year- round in conjunction with regular household chores, at a reduced level, to provide additional income for the household, or to cut back on supplies the family would need to purchase. Weaving could also be done at home for profit, although it typically was done on a more seasonal basis when the household workload allowed a woman time to spend a concentrated period working at the loom.

Spinning and weaving also fit within the traditional agricultural barter system; in this case an orphaned girl who was taught to spin or weave could further garner profit for her new family by using these new skills to assist a neighbor, thereby creating a credit for her family. Hand sewing, spinning and weaving also became more financially valuable skills as the putting out system became popular as part of the early factory system. Through this system orphaned girls would have been in a position to visibly contribute to the household economy.[11]

Theoretically other trades were open to orphan girls, but only if a master tradesman was willing to take on a young girl. Many tradesmen were unwilling to take on female apprentices, most likely because they did not want to break with standing gender norms and assumed that girls would be less capable of handling physical labor than boys. Not all master tradesmen felt this way; a very limited number did take on orphan girls as trade apprentices. To put these numbers in perspective, they are considered so rare as to be discounted from statistical studies as mere anomalies.[12] Yet for the few girls who were apprenticed out to printers, hat makers or other trades, they had the opportunity to learn skills that would allow them to profit later in life. Most of the girls who were bound out to a trade benefited from a living mother who arranged for the apprenticeship. In some cases mothers were able to take advantage of female masters when arranging apprenticeships, but the number of women who had mastered a trade and ran their own shops were also limited. Of the women who did run their own shops and took on orphan apprentices not all would take on female orphans; many elected to take male orphans instead, further limiting the options available to orphan girls. One notable example that does survive involving a female orphan being indented to learn a trade comes from Charleston, South Carolina. The girl's mother arranged the apprenticeship with the city's preeminent female merchant Margaret Moles, for her daughter to learn the trade of shop keeping. Had her mother not made these arrangements Sarah Fields would most likely have been apprenticed out to a textile trade, like so many other girls, rather than receiving a more extensive education in a trade that could potentially provide financial independence.[13]

Gender also played a role in where and to what types of families apprentices would be indented. There were two primary types of families that took in orphans - young rural families and wealthy urban families.[14] In order for a farm family to survive they had to produce a product for market, and this normally came in the form of surplus crops, which involved the employment of additional male labor.[15] Until a new couple produced children who grew old enough to assist on the farm, however, producing a crop surplus meant employing additional hands or bringing in an apprentice, in most cases an orphan apprentice. Most young couples preferred to bring on orphan apprentices because it cost less than hiring an adult, and the arrangement guaranteed year-round help. Besides the financial savings other factors went into choosing orphans over adults as well. Having a child in the house enabled the young couple to practice parenting skills, and demonstrate to the community that their own children would not go astray. Likewise it was considered a good sign to begin a marriage with an act of charity. Frequently bridegrooms would arrange the indentures prior to the marriage, and the children acted as wedding presents for their brides, helping to alleviate part of the work burden when the marriage began.[16] This is particularly true of orphan girls who were indented. While girls might not be able to add surplus crops to boost the family economy, they would have been able to assist with a substantial number of other chores, among them cooking, cleaning, caring for children, raising chickens, managing the kitchen garden and spinning wool. While any of these skills could be used to provide extra income to the family through the rural barter system the most valuable would have been spinning, which could have produced wool for market.[17] Most importantly, though, an orphan girl would have been valued on a rural farm for the assistance she provided the wife and mother of the family through the years of childbirth and rearing small children, a time when an extra pair of hands to help with food preparation or keep an eye on toddlers was invaluable.

Wealthy urban families would have brought in orphan indentures for different reasons. In most cases these were older, established families with grown children who could have afforded adult servants if needed.[18] The orphans were not brought in to provide the families with extra income but rather to showcase the wealth and Christian spirit of the family. Bringing in an orphan indenture demonstrated that the family could afford to keep the child, and it also demonstrated to the community that they were "Good Christians" because they took in a poor orphan to train rather than hiring an adult servant.[19] In return these orphans often performed basic chores that would have been done by the grown children that had now left the home, or assisted with increased demands in the household with the growing numbers of apprentices often associated with a successful business. While orphans may have been brought in to fill the spots left by the children of the family with regard to the household workload, it was rare for these children to be adopted into the families they worked for, or even to receive bequests upon their employer's death. Largely they remained additional, somewhat more reliable employees.[20] Due to the gendered nature of the work being performed in most urban households girls were often preferred to boys. Sarah Gillen apprenticed to John D. Taylor, a shoe manufacturer, fits perfectly into this case. Sarah, a New Jersey orphan, was indented not as a shoemaker's apprentice but to learn housewifery; in effect she was being brought on to help care for all the other apprentices and journeymen that Taylor would have needed to employ to keep his business running successfully.[21]

Just as gender played a role in where orphans were bound out, it also played a role in the frequency with which they were bound out. Girls tended to be bound out with a slightly lower frequency than boys. In some regions this may have been a result of skewed gender ratios among orphans, but most studies indicate that within populous areas boys and girls were brought to the attention of the Guardians of Poor or before the Orphans Court at a nearly equal rate.[22] The difference when it comes to indenting may be a result of the perceived value versus cost of care as related to boys versus girls. Social norms dictated a lower level of education and lower nutritional requirements for girls, who could also be trained in housewifery by any woman. Boys, on the other hand, required a higher level of education, more food (with larger quantities as they grew) and eventually training in a trade. As a result more girls were kept by relatives who still had young children, or reclaimed from orphanages by family members who could use additional hands in their own homes.[23]

The educational opportunities open to females in the eighteenth and nineteenth centuries varied by class, but throughout they remained fewer than those open to males. Those girls who belonged to the upper class had the most options available. They would be taught reading, writing and normally mathematics so they could manage household accounts. While more open minded families might allow their daughters to pursue advanced courses along with their sons, the majority would be limited to additional education involving ornamental skills such as dancing, drawing, music lessons and most importantly, needlework.[24] Those girls in the middle class would have learned many of the same basic skills as those in the upper class, but would not have had the opportunity to take any advanced courses and would have been limited to one or possibly two ornamental skills, predominantly needlework. Working-class girls had the fewest opportunities of all. While reading and writing were considered important for these girls by the middle of the nineteenth century, the opportunities for them to receive an education were still limited, and little thought had been given to the necessity of teaching these girls mathematics as well.[25] The biggest difficulty that working class, and to some extent middle class, girls faced was that most forms of schooling had to be paid for, and were charged at what we today consider higher per credit rates for those students who went part time, which most girls were required to do as a

Fig. 4.4 Writing was learned through repetition and grammar from books.

result of family income.[26] The few schooling options that did not require pay or were paid at a greatly reduced rate included the pauper schools and Sunday schools (See Fig. 4.4). Unfortunately these too had issues associated with them- pauper schools often had a separate track for girls, and accepted fewer students, and those that were accepted faced the social stigma of being branded a pauper. Sunday Schools met infrequently and only taught reading and possibly writing, provided they could find a teacher who was educated enough to perform that task.[27]

Orphan girls would originally have only had the opportunities open to girls of the working class. Once they entered the various welfare systems open to orphans during the eighteenth and nineteenth centuries, however, their options often increased. Orphanages, which still had higher standards for boys' education than girls' education, still provided their female residents with more schooling than they would have received at home.[28] Quaker schools also kept openings for pauper children and orphans, but once again they retained different standards for boys and girls, continually keeping the education available to girls one to two stages behind that of their male students regardless of what other advancements were made.[29] In many cases orphan girls' best chance for an education was actually being indented, especially as states began to standardize the practice. By the mid-nineteenth century New Jersey's Justices of the Peace were all using a standard form regardless of the orphan's gender to indent the child, one that required the same level of education for all orphans indented through the state's Orphan's Courts.[30]

Just as in education there were different standards for girls, there were also different standards for defining the success of female versus male orphans. Due to the stringent social restrictions placed on women in the eighteenth and nineteenth century success could not be defined through personal land or business ownership, nor rising to a leadership position in society as it was with male orphan; rather it had to be defined within acceptable gender norms, or in this case, the home. As a result orphan girls had their success defined by whom they married and the success of their husbands, not by their personal success.[31] A successful marriage could be achieved by marrying a man with property, even if he only had minimal property. Working class men by definition did not own property, and thus marrying someone with even minimal property rights meant moving socially upward. Another move was to marry a widower with substantial property and social position regardless of any age difference. Large age differences were common, especially in second marriages, and an orphan girl stood a greater chance of marrying up if she would not be the mother of the heir. One success story that we have involves Missouri Loper who married Philip R. Douglas, a slave owner with two hundred acres in 1838. Another story that survives comes from Mary Ann Kemp who married Augustus G. Boulineau, owner of a lumber business in 1829.[32]

Orphaned girls had limited opportunities for academic and trade education. The vast majority were sent into domestic service to conform to eighteenth and nineteenth century gender norms. Those who were given access to trade training were bound out to low paying textile trades. Without training in trades that were financially secure, orphan girls were forced to either marry or remain in menial jobs for the remainder of their lives. This dependence on marital success for financial security meant that few orphan girls would be defined by their personal successes. The cumulative effect of eighteenth and nineteenth gender stereotypes paired with the limited resources of many social welfare institutions of the period ultimately resulted in orphaned girls not reaping the same benefits from the binding-out system as orphaned boys.

Notes:
[1] John E. Murray, "Fates of Orphans: Poor Children in Antebellum Charleston," *The Journal of Interdisciplinary History* 33, no.4 (2003): 520.
[2] Monique Bourque, "Bound Out from the Almshouse: Community Networks in Chester County, Pennsylvania, 1800-1860," in *Children Bound to Labor: The Pauper Apprentice System in Early America*, ed. Ruth Wallis Herndon and John E. Murray (Ithaca: Cornell University Press, 2009), 83.
[3] Ruth Wallis Herndon, " "Proper" Magistrates and Masters: Binding Out Poor Children in Southern New England, 1720-1820," in *Children Bound to Labor: The Pauper Apprentice System in Early America*, ed. Ruth Wallis Herndon and John E. Murray (Ithaca: Cornell University Press, 2009), 50.; Karin L. Zipf, *Labor of Innocents: Forced Apprenticeship in North Carolina 1715-1919* (Baton Rouge: Louisiana State University Press), 37.

[4] Ruth Wallis Herndon, " "Proper" Magistrates and Masters: Binding Out Poor Children in Southern New England, 1720-1820," 48.; T. Stephen Whitman, "Orphans in City and Countryside in Nineteenth-Century Maryland," in *Children Bound to Labor: The Pauper Apprentice System in Early America*, ed. Ruth Wallis Herndon and John E. Murray (Ithaca: Cornell University Press, 2009), 57-58.

[5] Sharon Braslaw Sundue, *Industrious in Their Stations: Young People at Work in Urban America, 1720-1820* (Charlottesville: University of Virginia Press, 2009), 110.

[6] Adriana E. Van Zwieten, "Preparing Children for Adulthood in New Netherland," in *Children Bound to Labor: The Pauper Apprentice System in Early America*, ed. Ruth Wallis Herndon and John E. Murray (Ithaca: Cornell University Press, 2009), 91.

[7] Ibid., 91-92.

[8] Sundue, *Industrious in Their Stations*, 50-51.

[9] Gloria L. Mann, "Conclusion: Reflections on the Demand and Supply of Child Labor in Early America," in *Children Bound to Labor: The Pauper Apprentice System in Early America*, edited by Ruth Wallis Herndon and John E. Murray (Ithaca: Cornell University Press, 2009),206-210.

[10] One trade that orphan girls were indented to was manuta-maker, a type of dressmaker that would have required learning skills for constructing garments.; Timothy J. Lockley, " "To Train Them to Habits of Industry and Usefulness": Molding the Poor Children of Antebellum Savannah," in *Children Bound to Labor: The Pauper Apprentice System in Early America*, edited by Ruth Wallis Herndon and John E. Murray (Ithaca: Cornell University Press, 2009),145.

[11]Gloria L. Mann, "Conclusion: Reflections on the Demand and Supply of Child Labor in Early America," 206-210.

[12] WJ Rorabaugh did not include female apprentices in his book, *The Craft Apprentice: From Franklin to the Machine Age in America*, because he could not find indenture contracts for girls in trades other than "housewifery" or the textile industry. WJ Rorabaugh, *The Craft Apprentice: From Franklin to the Machine Age in America* (New York: Oxford University Press, 1986), viii.

[13] Murrary, "Fates of Orphans: Poor Children in Antebellum Charleston," 529-530.

[14] Barry Levy, "Girls and Boys: Poor Children and the Labor Market in Colonial Massachusetts," *Pennsylvania History* 64 (1997): 298-299.

[15] Ibid., 300.

[16] Ibid., 302.

[17] Sharon Braslaw Sundue, *Industrious in Their Stations: Young People at Work in Urban America, 1720-1820* (Charlottesville: University of Virginia Press, 2009), 24-25.

[18] Barry Levy, "Girls and Boys: Poor Children and the Labor Market in Colonial Massachusetts," 302.

[19] Ibid., 302.

[20] Sundue, *Industrious in Their Stations*, 43.

[21] Indenture of Sarah Gillen April 16, 1846. From the Collection of the Montclair Historical Society.; 1850 Federal Census, Courtesy of Ancestory.com.

[22] Ruth Wallis Herndon, " "Proper" Magistrates and Masters: Binding Out Poor Children in Southern New England, 1720-1820," 40.

[23] Monique Bourque, "Bound Out from the Almshouse: Community Networks in Chester County, Pennsylvania, 1800-1860," 81.; Sundue, *Industrious in Their Stations*, 42-43.

[24] Sundue, *Industrious in Their Stations*, 79.

[25] Ibid., 81-82.

[26] Ibid., 81-82.

[27] Ibid., 171-172.

[28] Ibid., 150.

[29] Ibid., 137-138.

[30] Child Indentures from the Collections of the Montclair Historical Society.

[31] Timothy J. Lockley, " "To Train Them to Habits of Industry and Usefulness": Molding the Poor Children of Antebellum Savannah," 144-145.

[32] While Kemp was able to enjoy her success Loper died young in 1845.; Ibid., 145.

5. ABOUT THE AUTHORS

Siobhan Fitzpatrick received her B.A. from Ramapo College and her M.A. in history from Villanova University. She has previously worked with the National Park Service and currently serves as the Curator of Collections and Exhibits for the Museum of Early Trades & Crafts in Madison, NJ.

Diane Marano received her B.A. from the University of Pennsylvania and her J.D. from Rutgers University Law School. She then went on to serve as Assistant Prosecutor in Camden County, NJ Prosecutor's Office, acting as Section Chief for the Juvenile Unit for over twenty years. She has since returned to the university and is working on her Ph.D. in Childhood Studies at Rutgers University, Camden.

Carol J. Singley received her B.A. and M.A. from Pennsylvania State University and her Ph.D. from Brown University. Currently she is an Associate Professor of English and Fellow at the Center for Children and Childhood Studies at Rutgers University Camden. Singley also directs the Undergraduate Liberal Studies program and co-directs the American Studies Program.

www.ingramcontent.com/pod-product-compliance
Lightning Source LLC
Chambersburg PA
CBHW041226270326
41934CB00001B/10